SRA Reading Mastery

Signature Edition

Picture Book for the Placement Test and the 15 Program Assessments

Siegfried Engelmann
Jean Osborn

McGraw Hill **SRA**

Columbus, OH

Table of Contents

Note: Show only one page of the Picture Book at a time.

Placement Test

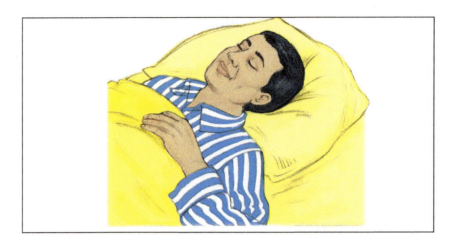

Part 1

Placement Test

Part 2

Assessment 1

Part C Object Identification

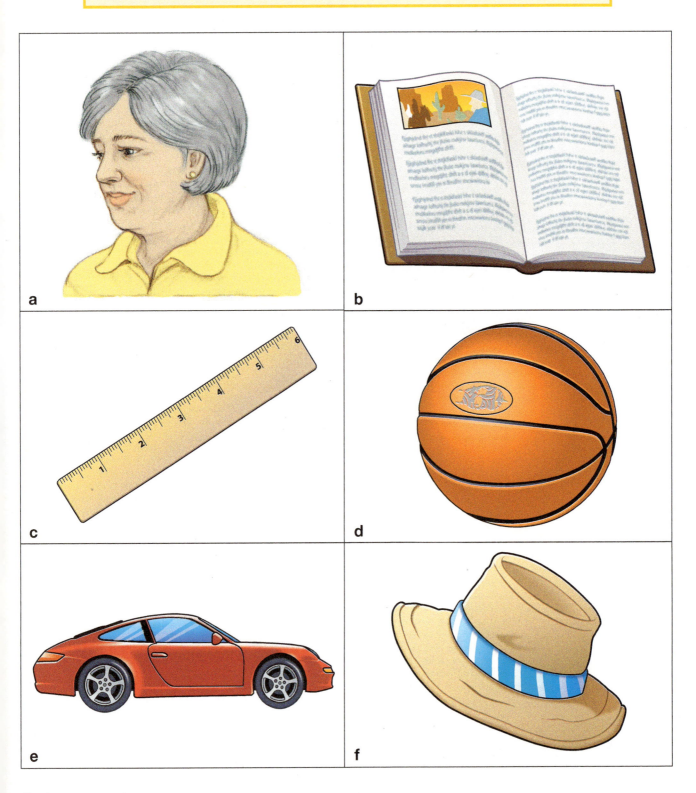

a

b

c

d

e

f

Assessment 2

Part D   Identity Statements

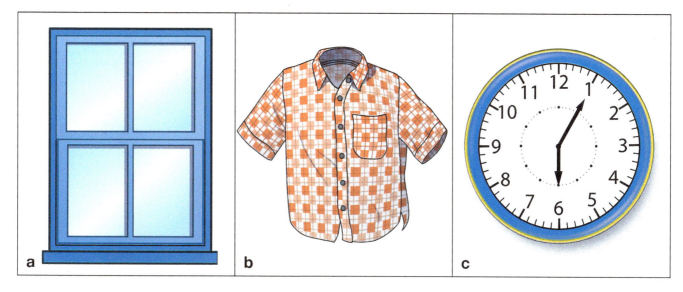

a   b   c

Part E   Action Statements

Part
B Identity Statements

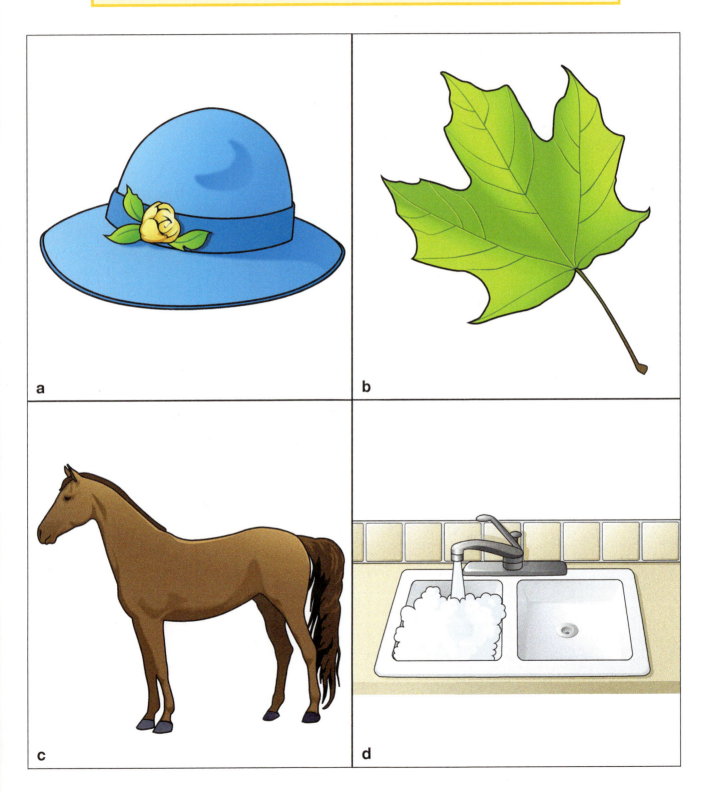

a

b

c

d

Assessment 3 (cont.)

After Lesson 30

Part C   Actions—First, Next

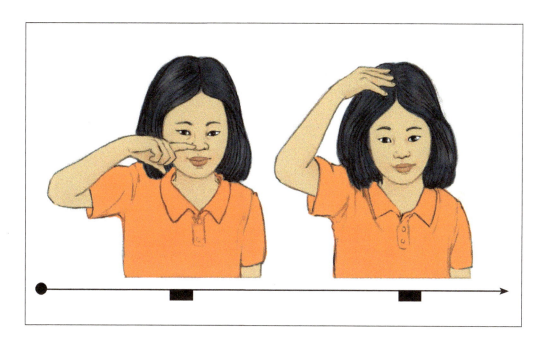

Part E   Action Statements

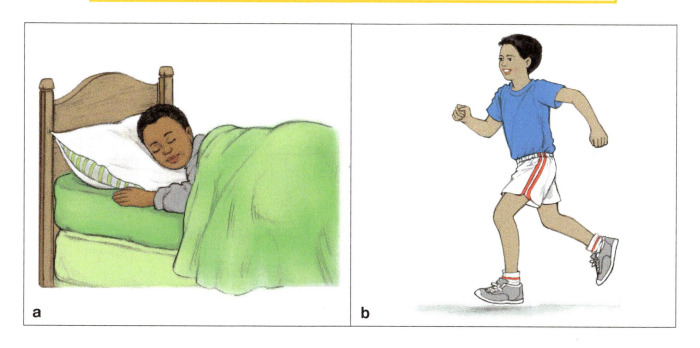

a   b

Assessment 4

Part C	Part/Whole

Part D	Prepositions

Part E	Opposites

Assessment 5

After Lesson 50

Part B Actions

Assessment 5 (cont.)

After Lesson 50

Part C   Opposites

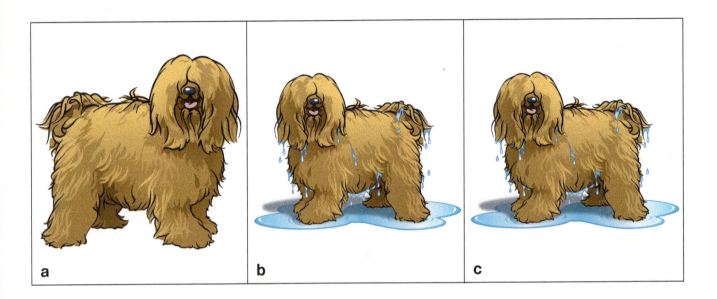

a   b   c

Part E   Part/Whole

Assessment 6

Part B Classification

a

b

Part E Concept Application

Assessment 6 (cont.)

Part E Concept Application (cont.)

Assessment 7

After Lesson 70

Part A   Part/Whole

Part C   Tense

a

b

Assessment 7 (cont.)

Part D	Classification

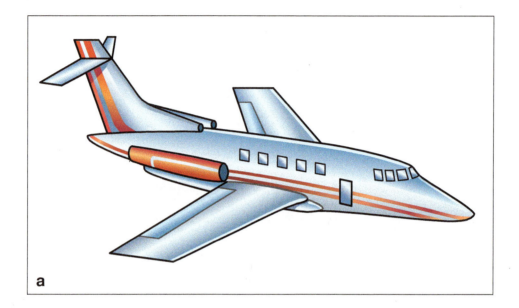

a

b

Assessment 7 (cont.)

After Lesson 70

Part F	Concept Application

Part	
F	Concept Application (cont.)

Assessment 8

After Lesson 80

Part B Tense

a

b

Part C Classification

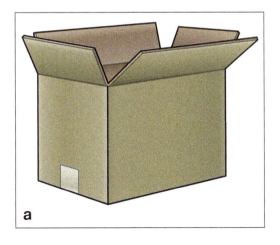

a

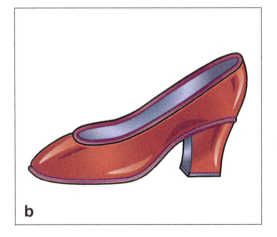

b

Assessment 8 (cont.)

After Lesson 80

Part D	Plural

Part E	Parts

Assessment 8 (cont.)

After Lesson 80

Part	
F	**Concept Application**

a   b   c

Assessment 9

Part E Classification

a

b

After Lesson 90

Part F Concept Application

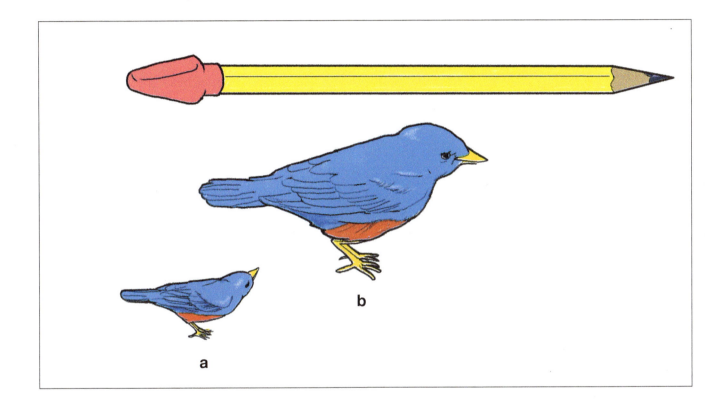

a

b

After Lesson 90

Part	
F	Concept Application (cont.)

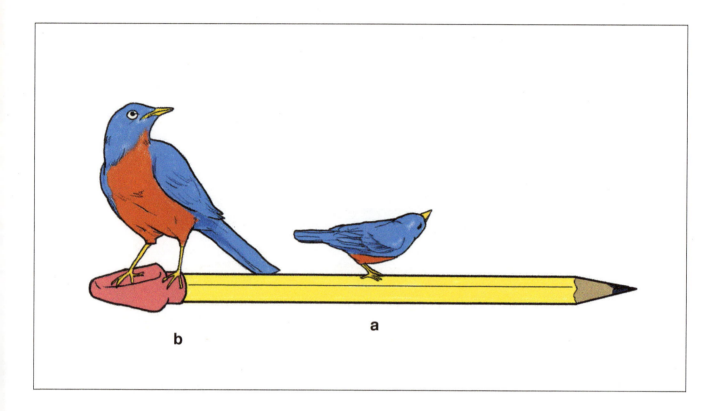

b

a

Assessment 10

After Lesson 100

Part	
C	**Tense**

a

b

After Lesson 100

Part E   Same

Part F	Concept Application

Part	
F	**Concept Application (cont.)**

Assessment 11

Part
D   Part/Whole

Part
G   Concept Application

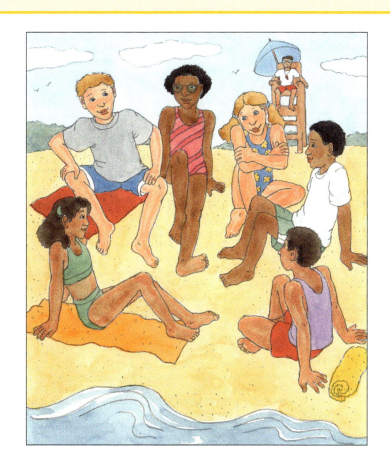

Assessment 11 (cont.)

After Lesson 110

Part G	Concept Application (cont.)

Assessment 12

After Lesson 120

> **Part C** Classification

Part D Before/After

Assessment 12 (cont.)

After Lesson 120

Part E	Concept Application
	Note: Do <u>not</u> show picture until item 36.

Assessment 13

After Lesson 130

Part
D Where, Who, When, What

Assessment 13 (cont.)

After Lesson 130

Part
E Classification

a

b

c

d

Assessment 14

Part C Comparatives

Part D Where, Who, When, What

Assessment 14 (cont.)

After Lesson 140

Part F Absurdities

a

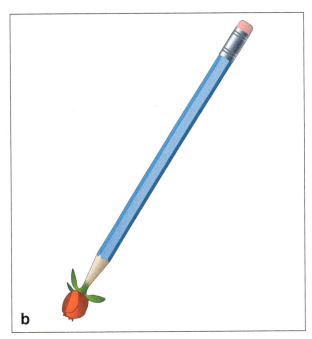

b

Part G Rules

Assessment 15

After Lesson 150

Part E **Absurdities**

Note: Do <u>not</u> show picture until item 37.

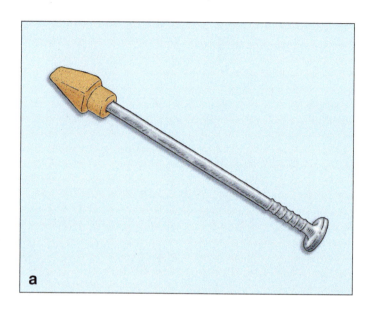

a

b

Assessment 15 (cont.)

After Lesson 150

Part F	Rules

Part H	Where, Who, When, What